BEHIND GOLD DOORS

FIVE EASY STEPS TO BECOME A WISDOM STEWARD

Lonnie Pacelli

Published by Pacelli Publishing
Bellevue, Washington

Pacelli
PUBLISHING

BEHIND GOLD DOORS
FIVE EASY STEPS TO BECOME A WISDOM STEWARD

Published by Pacelli Publishing
9905 Lake Washington Blvd. NE, #D-103
Bellevue, Washington 98004
PacelliPublishing.com

ISBN-13: 978-1-933750-54-5

Apollo

It was the toughest meeting in Rico's young career. He showed up at Alma's office ten minutes early. Her door was closed; he could hear muffled voices through the wall out into the hallway as she talked on the phone. Rico sat down in a chair outside her door, reminding him of when he would get sent to the principal's office in grade school. His right knee nervously bounced up and down as he gazed at his Birkenstocks. He'd been going over and over in his head how he was going to explain the slipped date and cost overrun. This was all foreign territory. In the five years since graduating college with a computer engineering degree he had consistently delivered results as an individual contributor. Then Alma gave him an assignment as a project manager leading a small team to deliver high-priority enhancements to their customer relationship management system.

Clients had been clamoring for these enhancements for months and the pressure was on to deliver.

Rico heard a muffled, "OK, let's talk again on Tuesday. Have a good weekend. Bye." Then the door opened. "Come on in, Rico."

He got up from the chair as Alma walked to a table in her office and sat in another chair across from him. She grabbed two waters from the mini-fridge.

"Thanks for seeing me, Alma," Rico said as she handed him a water bottle.

"Whew, it's a warm one today," Alma said as she pulled her hair back and tied it with an elastic band.

"I've lived here all my life and I still can't get used to these Phoenix summers. Have plans this weekend?" she asked.

"Um, not really." Rico wasn't much in the mood for idle chat. He twisted open his water and took a long gulp.

"So, let's talk about Apollo," Alma said. Rico named his project Apollo due to his fascination with Greek Mythology. His plan was to name all of his projects after Greek gods, but now he wasn't sure there would even be a next project.

"Did you see my status report?" Rico asked.

"I did. A two-month slip and a hundred grand over budget." Alma had a reputation for being an outstanding people cultivator; a number of her protégés had moved on to very significant roles in the company, thanks to her mentoring. She also was no-nonsense when it came to running her organization.

Rico looked down, not wanting to meet Alma's gaze. "Alma, I'm going to do everything I can to pull the date in as much as possible."

"I don't doubt you'll work 24/7 Rico," Alma said. "What happened?"

Rico then went into a long description about every detail which contributed to the project slippage. After about five minutes Alma interrupted him.

"OK, I heard you," Alma said as she took a sip of water. "When I first assigned the project to you, I asked you to use Tami as a coach since she's got a lot of experience with projects like this. Did you?"

Rico rubbed the back of his neck then rubbed his hand on his jeans to dry it off. "I tried to connect with her, but we just couldn't coordinate schedules."

Alma shook her head. "Sorry, Rico, but that's a baloney excuse. I asked you to talk with her for a reason. Tami's got a lot of experience on this type of work and could have helped avoid the slippage. Why didn't you talk with her?"

Rico looked at her, realizing that any more excuses would only get him in hotter water. "I've got nothing," he said.

"Rico, I gave you this project for a reason. I've been talking you up with my management as a rising star. Now I have to tell them that the project is not only coming in two months late but is 100K over budget. I know this meeting is uncomfortable for you, but the meeting I need to have this afternoon is going to be **very** uncomfortable for me."

"Gosh, Alma, I'm so sorry."

"I'm sure you are, but your apology won't make things any easier on me." As a seasoned people leader, Alma had been in this situation before. She knew the meeting with her management wouldn't be that bad, but she wanted to use the situation as a teachable moment for Rico.

"Rico, I need you to do two things for me; one, scrub the cost and schedule estimates to see where you can possibly bring things more back on track. And two, put together a one-page lessons-learned document on what went wrong and how you're going to avoid the same from happening to you in the future. It's a three-day weekend, so schedule some time on my calendar Tuesday morning to discuss both. OK?"

"OK, Alma."

"Good. You take care, Rico." Alma got up out of her chair. Rico got up and she patted him on the back as he left her office.

Rico slowly walked back to his cubicle, thinking about his two action items. Scrubbing the cost and schedule estimates was simply busy-work; he was comfortable doing the math and figuring out the revised project plan. It was the second one that was unfamiliar territory. He had created lessons-learned documents as part of a larger team on past projects. It was always the same; the team came up with a few "we should've done differently" items to appease management, then they went back to doing things the way they always did. This time it wasn't the team creating the lessons-learned; it was him documenting what *he* did wrong and what he learned from it. He also knew Alma would not put up with any blame shifting. It had to be about him or she'd make him go back and do it again. He picked up his phone and called his mother.

"Hey, Mom, can I come down this weekend?"

Sierra Vista

The Toltec exit was a familiar stopping point for Rico to use the facilities and get a soda. Having made the three-hour-plus trek from Phoenix to Sierra Vista dozens of times, he'd stop at his favorite fast-food joint about an hour into the drive. He stepped out of the car, feeling the heat from the blacktop through his sandals. In the dead of Summer, it never really cools off in the Arizona desert; it just vacillates between hot to searing hot. He got a diet cola and started back on the drive southeast.

Rico thought about the lessons-learned document he owed Alma. Admitting any kind of weakness was not in his lexicon; he always told others that failure was never an option. He was confident that it would never be him having to explain why something didn't go according to plan. *"Need to put on some tunes,"* he thought, trying to take his mind off things as he drove through Tucson on the way to Sierra Vista.

"Hi Mom, be there in about ten minutes," Rico texted as he passed the *Welcome to Sierra Vista* sign. The town's largest employer was Fort Huachuca, a U.S. Army post, having been operational since the late 1800s. Many who were stationed there stayed in the area after retirement, providing Sierra Vista with a rich population of both retired military and civil servants. Rico, his parents, and younger brother moved to Sierra Vista when Rico was still in high school. His parents decided to stay there after his dad retired from the Army as a lieutenant colonel. Rico went off to college at the University of Arizona then got a software engineering job in Phoenix after graduation. His father unexpectedly died shortly after he moved to Phoenix, the day after the two had a huge argument about Rico not calling him for his birthday . . . again.

"Family is important and you're alienating us. Stop being so self-centered," his father told him.

"Dad, you don't understand. My job is a grind. It just slipped my mind." The conversation ended abruptly with his father saying, "Think about what I told you." The next day he was dead. Rico had felt the guilt of his unresolved last conversation with his father ever since.

Rico could see his mother standing in the driveway as he pulled up. He barely got out of the car before she gave him a big hug.

"My beautiful boy!" she said as she wrapped her arms around him and kissed him on the cheek.

"Hey, Mom." Rico was never comfortable with her shows of affection, but since his father died, he had tried to show some grace.

"You hungry? I've got lunch waiting."

"Sure." Rico grabbed his duffel bag and followed her into the house. On the kitchen table there was a spread large enough to feed ten people. The two ate and made some small talk; his mother filled him in on all the goings-on with the extended family.

"You want to do anything this afternoon?" she asked.

"Actually, I think I'm going to take a walk. I've got some stuff to think through."

"OK," she said as she got up to clear the table. Rico grabbed some tennis shoes from his duffel and put them on.

"See you in a bit, Mom," Rico said as he headed out the front door.

"Have fun, honey," his mom yelled as she washed dishes.

Rico walked out the front door. The sun was shining just as brightly as in Phoenix, but the temperature was about ten degrees cooler; one of the attractions for the many people who decided to retire in Sierra Vista.

"Same old thing, house after house looks the same," Rico thought to himself as he passed each house painted in desert colors and Spanish-style red tile roofs. He was looking up at a tall palm with its green leaves fanned out toward the sky when he heard beeping behind him.

"Look out!"

Scorpion

He jumped out of the way just as the golf cart rolled past then screeched to a halt. Rico looked up to see the back of the driver, gripping the steering wheel with both hands, shoulders bobbing up and down in sync with each deep breath she took.

Rico ran up to the driver. "Are you OK?"

"It was a scorpion, I'm so sorry." She was a sixty-something woman with jet black hair pulled tightly into a bun. Her olive-toned complexion framed her sunken deep brown eyes. Her hands shook as she took them from the steering wheel.

"I looked down and saw a scorpion on the seat next to me. As I tried to brush it off I veered right into you. I could have killed you. I'm so so sorry, are you OK?"

"I'm fine," Rico said. "Are you?"

"I'll be OK in a bit; right now I'm pretty shaken up. I hate those scorpions!"

Rico had his own run-ins with the venomous insects through the years. "Me too. Are you OK to drive?"

"I-I'm not sure."

"Would you like me to drive you home?" Rico asked.

"Oh, I couldn't impose on you."

"Really it's no problem. I'm just out taking a walk. I'll drive you."

"Thank you so much, sir."

"Please, it's Rico."

"I'm Rachael," she said as she slid across the seat. Rico got into the driver's seat and put the golf cart in gear, which lunged forward as he hit the accelerator.

"Where do you live?" Rico asked.

"Oh, it's not far. What brings you here, Rico?"

"My mother lives here."

"Where do you live?"

"Phoenix. Used to live here."

"Nice to come back home. Here for a quick visit?"

"Just needed some relaxation time to do some thinking. Do I turn here?"

"No, just stay on this road for a while."

Rico wondered just how far away Rachael's place was and how long of a walk he'd have back to his mother's house. "OK," he said.

"What kind of thinking did you need to do?" Rachael asked.

"It's kind of a long story."

"We've got a bit of time," Rachael said. "What kind of thinking?"

Rico wasn't typically one to share with someone he just met, but for some strange reason he felt comfortable with this woman who nearly killed him just minutes ago.

"Well, I kind of got a spanking from my boss about my project and I have to come up with lessons learned about what went wrong and what I would do in the future to avoid making the same mistakes."

Rachael smiled. "Oh, I get it. Having to admit mistakes and what you've learned is always a hard thing to do. What kind of mistakes did you make?"

"Gosh, she's really showing a strong interest here," he thought. *"Guess there's no harm in sharing with her, it's not like she a competitor or colleague."*

"The one my boss brought up was me not talking with one of my colleagues who has a lot of experience with projects like mine."

"Sounds familiar. Reminds me of my early days at Argon."

"You were at Argon? What did you do?"

"I was the lead program manager for Atlas. You familiar with Atlas?"

"Who in business doesn't know about Atlas? Just the most used financial system in the world. Our company has been using it for years. I work on systems that interface with Atlas. You were the lead program manager on it?"

Rachael smiled. "Sure was, way back in the day. Had a team of over a hundred people working on it. I was a real hot shot, thought I could do no wrong, was determined to show all the more experienced guys how things were done. I ended up messing things up to a point where I almost got pulled from the project. Want to know what my problem was?"

"Definitely."

"I didn't take the time to learn from others. I thought I knew it all, that there was nothing I could learn from those more seasoned than me. Sounds like we may have a couple of things in common."

"This is way too weird," Rico thought.

"Take a right here," Rachael said.

"Check." Rico turned, the two leaning left as the golf cart careened to the right.

"Anyways, after I almost got axed, my manager and I had a heart-to-heart talk. She introduced me to a concept that has stuck with me ever since and changed how I work and live."

Rachael paused.

"What was it?" Rico asked in anticipation.

"Wisdom steward."

"Wisdom steward?" Rico asked.

"That's right."

"What's a wisdom steward?"

"There's my house on the left," Rachael said. "I hope your walk back isn't too far for you."

Hot Stove

Rico pulled into the driveway and stopped the golf cart. He turned to face her.

"Rachael, what's a wisdom steward?"

Rachael faced him and smiled.

"Do you really want to know?" Rachael asked.

"Yes."

"OK then." Rachael took a deep breath then continued. "First, let me ask you a question. Do you know the difference between knowledge and wisdom?"

"Aren't they the same thing?"

"Not quite, knowledge is facts and information learned through a number of sources. You can gain knowledge from a book, a discussion, the news, or personal experience. Wisdom is about what you do with that knowledge and the decisions you make as a result of your wisdom. You can't have wisdom without knowledge, but you can certainly have knowledge without wisdom."

"Sorry, what do you mean by that?" Rico asked.

"Let's look at touching a hot stove as an example. If you touch a hot stove with your hand, you gain the knowledge that the stove is hot and it will burn your hand. If you decide not to touch it again, then you're applying wisdom to knowledge to prevent getting burned again. However, if you do touch the stove and get burned again, you didn't apply wisdom to the knowledge you had. So, knowledge is knowing the stove is hot, wisdom is deciding to not touch it."

Rico paused, taking in the explanation. "So knowledge is having information and wisdom is knowing what to do with the information you have?"

"Exactly. Now let's talk about two ways to acquire wisdom. Wisdom can either be gained through first-hand experience or guided experience. First-hand experience is the stove example; I touched the stove, the stove is hot, I won't touch it again. Guided experience is gained through learning from others. Bill told me he touched the hot stove and burned his hand, so I won't touch the hot stove. You gained wisdom not because you did something first-hand, but because you learned from someone else's experience. In both cases you made a wise choice not to touch the stove, but in one you learned on your own and the other you learned from someone else. Make sense so far?"

"Sure."

"Now, how does this apply to a wisdom steward? For guided wisdom to work there must be two engaged parties. The first is the wisdom seeker. A wisdom seeker is humble and genuinely looks to gain wisdom from others to help him or her make a sensible decision. The second is the wisdom sharer. A wisdom sharer is transparent and candidly offers wisdom gained either first-hand or from others to help the seeker make a sensible decision. Take note of the words I'm using: a wisdom seeker is genuine and humble; a wisdom sharer is candid and transparent."

Rico shifted in the bench seat, turning toward Rachael, putting his right knee on the bench.

"Seeker and sharer, but how does this relate to a wisdom steward?" Rico asked.

Rachael smiled. "This is where the magic happens. A wisdom steward is both a seeker and sharer. In situations where the steward wants to learn from others, she genuinely and humbly learns from others who have wisdom to share. When a steward has an opportunity to share, she genuinely and transparently shares her wisdom, even if it means admitting a mistake."

That last part stung Rico. He always saw mistakes as a sign of weakness, and couldn't imagine sharing his mistakes to help others.

"Do you think you're a wisdom steward?" Rachael asked.

"Well, maybe," Rico said.

Rachael could see right through Rico. "You know, I've got five people that I think you should meet who can help you better understand wisdom stewardship. It'll only take a bit of time. Would you like to meet them?"

"Gosh I don't know, my mother is expecting me back home."

Just then Rico's phone rang. He looked at the incoming number.

"Hi Mom."

"Hi honey, I'm going to run a few errands this afternoon. Do you mind being on your own for a couple of hours?"

"Uh, sure Mom."

"Great, see you back at home."

"OK, bye."

Rachael looked at Rico and smiled. "Would you like to meet them?"

His one excuse now out the window, Rico relented. "Sure."

"Great! Switch spots with me," Rachael got out of the golf cart and walked around to the driver's side as Rico slid across to where Rachael was sitting.

"On we go!" Rachael shifted into reverse and the golf cart lunged backward down the driveway.

Hold On!

Rachael threw the golf cart in gear and hit the accelerator, jerking Rico's head back as the cart thrust forward.

"Wow, these things really do have some pep," Rico said.

"Sure do," Rachael said as the golf cart made its way down the street.

Rico looked over at Rachael, both hands gripped on the steering wheel, head forward, eyes fixed straight ahead.

"What a quirky lady," he thought as they drove down the street passing house after house. *"Did my mother put her up to this? Is it all just a strange coincidence?"*

"We'll be at the first house in a minute," Rachael said. "Can you grab the clipboard in my bag behind you?"

"Sure." Rico reached behind him into a canvas bag where he felt the metal clip on the clipboard.

"Got it?"

"Yes." Rico looked at the single sheet of paper on the clipboard:

PERSONA	CHARACTER TRAITS	WHEN IS THIS ME?	WHAT WILL I DO ABOUT IT?
STEWARD – EMBRACING SUCCESS	• GENUINELY SEEKS • CANDIDLY SHARES		

BECOMING A WISDOM STEWARD

THE STEPS:
1.
2.
3.
4.
5.

"Good. Now let me explain what you're looking at. The top section will be where you write down the wisdom personas of the people you're going to meet. I started the first one for you, which is the wisdom steward persona. I also put down the character traits of a wisdom steward: genuinely seeks and candidly shares. For each of the other personas you meet, you'll write down the persona name and the character traits of that persona. Hold on!"

Rachael swerved around the corner, the two of them leaning right as she took the hard turn left.

"The bottom section is the steps you will go through to become a wisdom steward. Each of the five people you'll visit will talk about one of the steps."

"What about the 'When is this me?' and 'What will I do about it?' columns up top?" Rico asked.

"Bob will explain those to you. Here we are!" Rachael pulled into the driveway of what looked like a typical beige house with a red tiled roof and desert-landscaped yard. What was peculiar about the house was the front door. It was a bright gold wooden door with a large brass ring door knocker at its center.

"I've been around this neighborhood for years and seen this house hundreds of times; odd I never noticed the door--must be new." Rico thought.

"You're going to notice a lot of things today, Rico," Rachael said.

"Wait, you heard my thoughts?"

Rachael smiled at Rico. "Off you go now, I'll be here when you get back."

"Uh, OK." Rico got out of the golf cart and walked to the front door. He turned back to Rachael who flicked her hands directing him to go to the door. Rico grabbed the brass ring and knocked on the door. The door swung open.

"Come in, Rico."

Bob the Boaster

Rico stepped over the door threshold into the house.

"I'm in the kitchen," the man yelled.

Rico walked along the burnt orange terra-cotta floor, by the living room with only a chair and TV, then into the kitchen. A man with a shaved head and a gray bushy unkempt beard sat at the kitchen table.

"Please sit, Rico," the man said.

Rico went to the kitchen table and sat down.

"Are you Bob?" Rick asked.

"I am. Would you like a water?"

"Actually, yes." Bob got up and poured two glasses of water from the kitchen tap and put them on the table.

"You drink tap water?" Rico always hated the mineral-like taste of Arizona water, opting for bottled water instead.

"I do. I don't want to pay for any of that frou-frou water when I can get it free from the tap." Bob took a swig of the warm, bitter water.

"Ah, good water," Bob said.

Rico looked at the slightly cloudy glass of water in front of him. *"Think I'll pass,"* he thought to himself.

"If you were dying of thirst in the desert that glass of water would look awfully good."

Rico looked at Bob. "Wait, you can hear my thoughts?"

Bob smiled as he took another sip.

"I heard about your meeting with your boss. Been there way too many times myself."

"How did you know about my meeting?"

"Rachael told me about it and asked me to chat with you."

"When did she talk with you?"

"Earlier this morning."

"Wait, I just met her a few minutes ago. How . . .?"

Bob put up his hand. "It'll all make sense in time. Now tell me about your meeting."

"Well, my boss raked me over the coals about my project being behind schedule and over budget."

"She raked you over the coals?"

Rico paused. "Um, not really raked, I guess."

"So, she talked with you about your project being behind schedule and over budget, right?"

Rico looked down. "Yeah, I guess you could say talked not raked."

"So what was the outcome?"

"She asked me to think about what went wrong and what I would do differently in the future."

"Did she point anything out to you?"

"Well, she asked why I didn't use one of my colleagues as a coach."

Bob smiled. "So that's why Rachael wanted me to talk with you."

"Why?" Rico asked.

"Did she talk with you about being a wisdom steward?"

"She did, then gave me this clipboard that I'm supposed to fill out or something."

Bob took another sip of water. "Let me tell you a bit about me. Was a public utilities field service engineer my entire career, hired right out of college. I was a real hot shot, thought I knew everything. My first supervisor told me I needed to do better at listening to others. So that's what I did. I listened to others, but then used that as an opportunity to prove them wrong in what they were thinking. Even when someone asked me my opinion on something, I only gave it to show him or her how smart I was. Behind my back they started calling me Bob the Boaster, because I was all about proving superiority. This continued on until that horrible day."

"What happened?"

"I nearly blew up a school."

"What?"

"That's right." Bob paused for a moment. "I had a great idea for what I thought was an innovative electrical design for a new building. A couple of my colleagues who reviewed the design told me that it wouldn't work under heavy load. Me and my superiority didn't listen. I implemented the design, then shortly after the school opened a fire broke out in the basement. Got all the kids out and the fire department got there just in time before the place would have gone up in flames. It scared me to death and got me assigned to a desk job working for a very direct but understanding new boss. I pushed paper for a year which gave me plenty of time to think about what happened. My boss and I had a number of discussions about how my boastful attitude nearly got a bunch of kids killed and how I needed to make some changes if I ever wanted to go out in the field again. She told me I had to be willing to seek and share wisdom without an ulterior motive to prove my own superiority. I didn't realize it at the time, but she was talking about being a wisdom steward. Are you a boaster, Rico?"

Rico looked down at the still-cloudy glass in front of him. "I don't think so."

"That didn't sound like a convicted statement," Bob said.

"Uh, I suppose there have been times that I asked questions just to prove I knew a lot about something."

"Ah, so it wasn't about wanting to learn, it was about wanting to teach, right?"

"When you put it that way, then I guess you can say that."

"So let me tell you what I did about it. I pinned the newspaper headline about the school incident to the inside of my cubicle and wrote 'NO BOASTING' across the top. I then made it a goal to self-assess when I thought I was being a boaster. I had to be very honest with myself which was really hard for me. It's always tough for a boaster to admit to doing something wrong, which is why I put the newspaper headline in my cubicle as a reminder of what my boasting nature could have caused. It was a lot of work, but I ultimately got there. I eventually moved back into the field and finished out my career. I slowly changed my reputation and became known as someone who genuinely seeks wisdom and candidly shares. I've talked to many groups about the school incident, what I did wrong, and what they could learn from the situation. It eventually became second nature to me and I even took to coaching other boasters on how to become stewards. I guess you could say I took a potentially disastrous situation as a learning opportunity to help others be better. It's just a blessing no one was hurt because of my foolishness."

"I can see that," Rico said as he took a tiny sip of the water. *"Still tastes horrible,"* he thought.

"You get used to it," Bob said. "Now about the clipboard."

Rico looked down at the clipboard and the writing on it.

"See in the top section the column that's titled Personas?" Bob asked.

"Yup."

"Rachael put the steward persona down and defined it as 'embracing success'. How would you describe the persona we just talked about?"

"I'd say the persona is 'boaster' and the definition is 'proving superiority,' right?"

"Exactly. Now look at the steward's character traits. What did Rachael write?"

"Genuinely seeks and candidly shares," Rico said.

"Good, so what would you say the character traits are for a boaster?"

"I'd have to say seeks and shares to demonstrate superiority to others."

"Sounds right to me," Bob said. "Now at the bottom section of the page you see 'The Steps'?"

"I do."

"What did I tell you I had to do to help me change from boaster to steward?"

"You openly and honestly assessed your behaviors," Rico said.

"I did. That's the first step in becoming a wisdom steward. As you self-assess, you'll write down when you are being a boaster to help you break boasting habits and become a wisdom steward. How about you write down what we just discussed?"

Rico unclipped the pen from the clipboard and wrote the boaster persona definition and characteristics and the first step to become a wisdom steward:

BECOMING A WISDOM STEWARD

PERSONA	CHARACTER TRAITS	WHEN IS THIS ME?	WHAT WILL I DO ABOUT IT?
STEWARD – EMBRACING SUCCESS	• GENUINELY SEEKS • CANDIDLY SHARES		
BOASTER – PROVING SUPERIORITY	• SEEKS AND SHARES TO DEMONSTRATE SUPERIORITY TO OTHERS		

THE STEPS:

1. DEFINE "WHEN IS THIS ME?"
2.
3.
4.
5.

"There are four more persona boxes and four more steps. Let me guess, four more people to talk to?" Rico asked.

"Quick study," Bob said. "You've got a lot to go, so you better get a move-on. Embrace the journey, Rico."

"Thank you, Bob." Bob and Rico got up from the table and Bob led him to the gold door.

"This is really going to freak him out," Bob thought as he opened the door.

Herman the Hoarder

The door opened.

"Huh?" Rico said as he looked out the door, expecting to see the sunny outside, but facing a dark, dated living room instead. He looked over at Bob, who was smiling as he held the door open.

"Off you go, Rico," Bob said as he motioned Rico out the door. Rico tentatively stepped across the threshold, giving Bob one last glance as he passed through. The door slammed shut behind him.

A gray-haired man wearing a long-sleeved collared shirt and yellow and gray argyle vest sat in a plush camel recliner.

"Are you Rico?" The man said in a weak, high-pitched voice.

"Yes," Rico said as he looked around at the room, with its brown shag carpeting and beige walls. A picture of the man with a woman and three children hung on the wall to his left. An entertainment center stood in the right corner of the room containing a 19-inch television and a rack full of audio components. A wooden tower with neatly stacked records, cassettes, and 8-tracks was to the left of the entertainment center.

"Please sit down," the man said, pointing to a flowered upholstered chair across from him.

Rico slowly walked to the tower and looked at the 8-tracks, noticing them to be in alphabetical order by artist.

"You like The Doors?" Rico asked.

"Love them. Morrison died too young; one of the 27 club."

"I know. I loved Cobain and Winehouse. All gone too soon."

"Who?" the man asked.

"You don't know Kurt Cobain and Amy Winehouse? They died in 1994 and 2011."

The man smiled. "Oh yeah, the future."

"Future?" Rico asked.

"That's right."

Rico walked to the chair. "What year is this?"

"1980."

"'80?"

"Perhaps you should sit. My name is Herman."

Rico lowered himself into the chair, his hands gripping the wooden armrests as he sat.

"Can I get you a Dr. Pepper?" Herman asked.

"I haven't had a Dr. Pepper in years. Love one."

Herman got up, went into the kitchen and put two sodas and two foil-wrapped pucks on the table between them.

"Ding Dongs?"

"Of course," Herman said as he pulled the foil from the cake and took a bite. "Ding Dongs and Dr. Pepper. Best afternoon snack. Go ahead, take one."

Rico picked up the other Ding Dong, took off the foil, and broke it in half, looking at the white creamy filling surrounded by the dark chocolate outer shell. He put half in his mouth and closed his eyes as he chewed.

"Mmm, better than my normal kale chips snack," Rico said.

"Kale chips? You eat kale chips in the future? Yeah, and I'll bet you eat seaweed in the future too," Herman said sarcastically.

"Well, actually . . ."

"Ugh, never mind," Herman said as he took a last bite. "Did you have a good visit with Bob?"

"I suppose. Freaked me out that I walked right into your place from his."

"Happens every time," Herman said as he took a sip. "I love seeing the reaction on faces when they expect to be going outside but come into my house instead. Never gets old."

"Uh, I suppose."

"Well, I've got to keep to schedule, so how about we get into it? I worked as an insurance salesman for years before I retired back in '72. Won best salesman of the year more than anyone else in the company. Really knew how to get customers to buy our most profitable products. I learned from the very best salespeople how to gain the customer's trust and get them to buy."

"Sounds like you were very successful," Rico said.

"In some respects, yes. I made the company a lot of money. I didn't flaunt my awards with the rest of the team. I was very open to seeking the wisdom from others to help me be a better salesperson. Yet there was this wedge between me and the rest of the sales team. For the longest time I didn't understand it."

Rico took a drink of the soda.

"Did Bob try to pawn tap water off on you?" Herman asked.

Rico laughed. "He did."

"That cheapskate. Won't even spend money on good water. Anyway, back to me. A new manager took over the department who was one of the best people managers I've ever seen. She could read her team and diagnose what was working and what wasn't. She sat me down and pointed out something I never even considered."

"What's that?" Rico asked.

"She told me about the importance of not only seeking wisdom but also sharing wisdom. I was great at wanting to learn from others so I could be a better salesperson, but I was unwilling to share wisdom with others to help them be better. She told me I was a wisdom hoarder."

"Wisdom hoarder?"

"That's right. I would genuinely seek wisdom from others but when it came to sharing, I was very guarded."

"Why were you guarded?" Rico asked as he popped the rest of the cake in his mouth, then licked the melted chocolate from his fingers.

"Honestly, part of it was just not thinking it was important to do. Another part of me was being competitive; I felt if I shared my secrets that others would be as good as or, even worse, better than me. In my mind, protecting what I knew helped ensure I would continue winning awards and praise from management."

Rico looked down at the clipboard at the wisdom steward character traits. "So, you did half of what a wisdom steward does, which is to genuinely seek, but instead of candidly sharing you were guarded about what you shared, right?"

"Precisely."

"So what did you do about it?"

"Great question, and this gets into the second step of becoming a wisdom steward. It wasn't enough for me to self-assess when I was being a hoarder. I had to get coaching from my manager and two peers who would supportively speak the truth to me. They regularly met with me to help me understand situations where I had opportunities to candidly share wisdom but didn't. I also had to change my attitude about competing with my peers. I won't lie to you; it was really difficult for me to do. Over time, though, I learned that being willing to candidly share wisdom helped in my relationships with others, both inside and outside of my work life. I was viewed as more authentic; that I was willing to share not just my successes but my failures to help others be better. Now let me ask you, Rico. Are you a wisdom hoarder?"

Rico paused for a moment. "No," he stammered.

Herman smiled. "Exactly the same response I gave to my manager. She smiled at me and asked me to start taking notes on situations where I could have shared wisdom but didn't. It took me a couple of months before I started noticing my hoarding tendencies. Perhaps you should do the same. Can you at least commit to taking notes on yourself?"

"I guess," Rico said as he nervously took a sip of soda.

"That's about as good as I could hope. Now how about you write down what we discussed?"

Rico unclipped the pen from the clipboard and wrote the hoarder persona definition and characteristics and the second step to become a wisdom steward:

BECOMING A WISDOM STEWARD

PERSONA	CHARACTER TRAITS	WHEN IS THIS ME?	WHAT WILL I DO ABOUT IT?
STEWARD – EMBRACING SUCCESS	• GENUINELY SEEKS • CANDIDLY SHARES		
BOASTER – PROVING SUPERIORITY	• SEEKS AND SHARES TO DEMONSTRATE SUPERIORITY TO OTHERS		
HOARDER – BEING COMPETITIVE	• GENUINELY SEEKS • GUARDEDLY SHARES		

THE STEPS:
1. DEFINE "WHEN IS THIS ME?"
2. REVIEW "WHEN IS THIS ME?" WITH UP TO 3 SHARERS
3.
4.
5.

"Well, it's about time for you to leave. Want to take your Dr. Pepper with you?" Herman said as he got up from his chair.

"That's OK." Rico put the soda can and foil wrapper down on the table as he stood up.

Herman walked Rico to the front door. "There's no easy path to success, Rico."

Herman extended his hand.

"Bye Herman," Rico said as he shook Herman's hand.

Herman opened the front door to a bright orange sun along the ocean's horizon. A woman sat on the beach in a blue lounge chair enjoying the sunset. Rico stepped out the door onto the sand.

"The boy's got a lot to learn," Herman thought as he closed the door.

Priscilla the Poser

R ico could feel the heat through his tennis shoes as he walked across the hot sand. He approached the woman, her eyes closed, smiling as the warm evening sun beat down on her. Her dark hair was contrasted by gray highlights that framed her porcelain-white complexion. She opened her eyes just as he got to her.

"Sorry I don't have another chair. Are you OK sitting on a beach towel?"

"Uh, yeah."

"Good, there's one in my bag. Go ahead and spread it out."

Rico looked back. His footstep trail led to a bungalow on the beach with the same gold door he saw on Bob's and Herman's house. He reached into her bag and pulled out a blue and red striped beach towel. The wind unfolded the towel as he held one end and set it on the sand.

"I love the sunsets. It's the only time I can be on the beach when it's light out, my skin being so fair and all. Do you like beach sunsets?"

"Honestly, I haven't spent much time on the beach." Rico said as he lowered himself onto the towel.

"Ah, a desert boy, huh?"

"Yup, born and raised in Arizona."

"You're Rico, right? My name is Priscilla."

"How do they all know my name?" He thought.

"Rachael told us about you."

"There's that mind reading thing again." Rico thought as Priscilla smiled at him.

"How has your visit been so far?"

"Honestly, surreal."

"I know. I felt the same way when I sat on the beach towel you're sitting on now."

"This happened to you too?" Rico asked.

"It did. Back when I was a young consultant."

"Did you meet Rachael, Bob, and Herman?"

"I did. They haven't aged a day. Paula used to do my job, sitting right here in this very chair, talking to people like you. She made a huge impression on me. When she decided to retire, Rachael asked me if I would like to take her place. I jumped at the opportunity, hoping to help people in the same way Paula had helped me."

"Speaking of Rachael, where is she?" Rico asked.

"Probably speeding around in her golf cart. She loves that thing. Did she almost hit you?"

"She did." Rico said.

"Ah, still uses that ploy; almost runs over you, then is too shaken to drive home, right?"

"She did that to you too?"

"The very same thing," Priscilla dug her feet in the sand. "I've got just a few minutes with you, so how about we get into why you're here?"

"I'd love to know why I'm here," Rico said as he looked up and down the pristine beach. It was just him and Priscilla as far as the eye could see.

"Very well then. Right after college I went to work as a consultant. It was typical for my company to oversell our skills to justify a higher billing rate. It was the same story at every client: arrive at the client site and do everything I could to learn as fast as I could about the client, the industry, the business environment. At the same time the client was expecting that I had the required expertise to help them with their problem. I, along with my peers, had to learn quickly about things I was expected to know without tipping the client off. As a consultant, I was expected to know everything, and saying 'I don't know' was a major no-no. Consequently, I built some very bad habits about seeking and sharing wisdom, which ultimately got me kicked out of a client."

"How so?" Rico asked.

"I was working with a client who was very experienced in her job. I was asked to help her do her job more efficiently. I made some recommendations to her based on a narrow understanding of what she did and some best practices I read about. As she started asking me questions about my recommendations it became evident to her that I really didn't know what I was talking about; that what I knew was no more than what anyone could have read about on the internet. After a torturous hour she ended the meeting and told her boss that I shouldn't be working at the client. I was gone by close of business."

"Ouch! That had to hurt," Rico said.

"It was a huge ego blow and I wanted to quit. A friend suggested I take a couple of days off to clear my head. I decided to visit my folks in Sierra Vista. One afternoon when I was out walking, Rachael almost ran me over, then I met Paula, who helped me understand something about myself that I needed to change."

"And what was that?"

"That I was a wisdom poser."

"A wisdom poser?" Rico asked.

"A wisdom poser."

"What's that?"

"Look, isn't the sunset beautiful?" Priscilla asked as the sun lowered behind the ocean, sending an orange trail across the water.

Rico nodded his head, waiting for her answer.

"Sorry, I just get so distracted by the beauty of it all. Your question again, Rico?"

"What's a wisdom poser?"

"Right. You're familiar with how a wisdom steward embraces success by genuinely seeking and candidly sharing wisdom, right?"

"Yup."

"Good. A wisdom poser's primary motivation isn't about embracing success. The poser is concerned with impressing others. I was all about impressing my client. So, I would guardedly seek wisdom without exposing how much I didn't know. My motive was to understand enough so I could dazzle others with my command of subject matter. The problem was that my wisdom on many topics wasn't wisdom at all; it was something I read or briefly talked with someone about. So, when I started getting questioned about topics I would profess to have expertise in, I would get myself in trouble. Now, I could very easily blame my bosses for overselling me, but then I'd be in denial about some character flaws I needed to address. Paula helped point out to me that at times I was a poser. I'm so thankful she did because I became a much better consultant as a result."

Rico was silent as he looked over at the almost disappearing sun, absorbing what Priscilla had said.

"Talk to me, Rico."

Rico paused a moment. "It's just that poser is such a harsh word; it makes it sound like I'm faking it."

"That may be true, but try to not miss the forest for the trees. The goal is to help you become a wisdom steward. Getting there means you need to admit to yourself how you act under certain situations, so you know what your starting point is. If you know your starting point and your goal, then you can more clearly define what to do to reach your goal. Which brings me to the third step to become a wisdom steward: defining how to change habits so you can genuinely seek and candidly share wisdom."

"This is getting really tough," Rico said.

"I know how you feel, Rico. When I embarked on the wisdom steward journey it was extremely uncomfortable. I had to not only be very honest with myself but had to hear some hard messages from the three people I asked to help me. There was more than one time I wanted to go home and cry, but I heard Paula's voice saying, 'You've got this' over and over. I'm glad I stuck with it. You've got this, Rico."

"I don't know."

Priscilla got up from her chair, crouched in front of Rico, grabbed his shoulders, and looked into his eyes. "Rico, you've got this."

"Thank you, Priscilla."

"Now, while it's fresh in your mind, how about you take out your clipboard."

Rico took the pen from the clipboard and wrote the poser persona definition and characteristics and the third step to become a wisdom steward:

BECOMING A WISDOM STEWARD

Persona	Character Traits	When is this me?	What will I do about it?
STEWARD – EMBRACING SUCCESS	• GENUINELY SEEKS • CANDIDLY SHARES		
BOASTER – PROVING SUPERIORITY	• SEEKS AND SHARES TO DEMONSTRATE SUPERIORITY TO OTHERS		
HOARDER – BEING COMPETITIVE	• GENUINELY SEEKS • GUARDEDLY SHARES		
POSER – NEEDING TO IMPRESS	• GUARDEDLY SEEKS WITHOUT EXPOSING SELF • SHARES WITHOUT BASIS		

THE STEPS:

1. DEFINE "WHEN IS THIS ME?"
2. REVIEW "WHEN IS THIS ME?" WITH UP TO 3 SHARERS
3. DEFINE "WHAT WILL I DO ABOUT IT?"
4.
5.

"I think it's about time for your next appointment, Rico. Remember, you've got this."

Rico got up and started folding the towel.

"Oh, don't worry about that, I'll get it later," Priscilla said.

"Thanks," Rico said as he laid the towel back out across the sand. "Do I go back to the cabana?"

"Yes, right through the gold door. Be well, Rico."

"Bye." Rico walked to the gold door at the cabana, turning to see Priscilla lying on the beach towel, hands behind her head, a smile on her face.

Helen the Hesitator

Rico opened the cabana's gold door to a harbor bustling with people. He shook the sand from his tennis shoes as he stepped onto the blacktop. He saw a woman sitting at a small orange table waving at him. As he walked to her, he caught the scent of salmon grilling at a street vendor's booth. A large Ferris wheel was off in the distance. It was the strange statue, though, that got his attention.

"Hello Rico!" The woman said as he approached the table.

"Um, where am I and is that statue what I think it is?"

The woman laughed. "Yes, it always gets a reaction the first time people see it. My name is Helen, please sit!"

Rico sat on a small orange metal bistro chair, never taking his gaze off the pink statue.

"Where am I?" he asked.

"That statue is called Bad Bad Boy. He's about 30 feet tall. And yes, he is peeing."

"Wait, I've heard about that statue. I'm in Helsinki?"

"You are. Some of the most beautiful summers on earth. The people here are so kind. Most everyone speaks English. And the best cardamom rolls anywhere! Would you like one with a cappuccino?"

"Eh, sure."

Helen got up and went to a street vendor selling coffee and rolls. Rico looked up and down the Bay of Finland, the deep blue water, the throngs of people enjoying boat rides and street food. Helen returned to the table with two cappuccinos and cardamom rolls.

"Here we are," she said as she put the cups and rolls on the table.

"Thank you," Rico said as he picked up a roll and took a bite.

"What do you think?" Helen asked.

Rico slowly chewed, taking in the flavor and texture of the roll.

"Unique, kind of like ginger, cloves and cinnamon. Not too sweet. Really like that they're not slathered in icing."

"Follow it up with a sip of cappuccino. It's heavenly." Helen took a bite followed by a quick slurp. She closed her eyes. "Heavenly."

"What's that out there?" Rico said as he pointed out to a cluster of islands in the middle of the Bay.

"Ah, that's Suomenlinna. The Finns call it The Sea Fortress of Helsinki. It was built in the 18th century when Finland was part of the Swedish Kingdom. It was taken over by the Russians in 1808 when, a year after, Russia made Finland an autonomous state and called it The Grand Duchy of Finland. In 1917 Finland gained its independence from Russia. It remained an active military fortress until 1972. Now it's one of the most popular tourist attractions in Finland. I wish we had time to go there then take a sauna."

"A sauna?" Rico asked.

"Yessir. Saunas are very popular here. There are 1.5 million saunas in Finland, even though the country only has five million people. They're commonplace in homes and businesses. In the winter, Finns go into a superheated sauna then jump into an icy lake. I haven't quite gotten into that custom."

"I think that would put my Arizona blood into shock," Rico said as he took another bite.

"I tried it once. Even my Chicago blood couldn't handle it."

"You're from Chicago? How'd you get here?"

"I worked for a gaming company that developed a strategic partnership with the company that created Angry Birds. You familiar with Angry Birds?"

"Yup. I try to stay away from it or I'll spend hours playing."

Helen laughed. "I know, it's addictive. Anyway, I spent a year working here on the strategic partnership before retiring. I fell in love with the city so decided to stay here. Summers are best. Winters get a bit long and dark, but I just accept it as part of the Helsinki experience."

"Good attitude," Rico said.

"Thanks. I enjoyed a long and fruitful career in the gaming industry and saw so much change since starting way back in the '70s. I've also grown a lot as a professional and person, particularly in how I seek and share wisdom."

Helen took a quick sip and continued. "I've always struggled with self-confidence, even back to my days in grade school. I seemed to always know the answers but was afraid to raise my hand and speak up. I was the quiet kid who didn't say much in class but got straight As. It got a bit better as I grew up, but when I started working after college it seemed to get worse. In meetings I would just keep to myself while my colleagues fought to command the stage. Most times I was spot-on with what I was thinking but no one knew it because I didn't speak up. It wasn't until my manager and mentor Ann intervened."

"How so?" Rico asked.

"Ann was an outstanding manager and really worked to draw people out and get them to express themselves. During a one-on-one meeting she asked me why I didn't speak up more. I told her that I always struggled with self-confidence and that I was concerned what others would think of my views. 'I completely relate,' she said. She then talked to me about the concept of seeking and sharing wisdom, that I was great at genuinely seeking wisdom but that I was hesitant to share wisdom unless it felt safe to do so. 'Helen, this will be career limiting unless you work on it,' she said. 'We need to get you comfortable with sharing wisdom and not being concerned about what others think of your ideas. We need to grow you from a hesitator to a steward.'"

"A hesitator?"

"That's what she said. And after she pointed it out to me, I started noticing how much wisdom I really had that I didn't share, and how it was bad not only for me but for others I worked with. The watershed moment for me was when I helped another team member bring a project back from life support. His acknowledgement of me with my peers on how I helped him be successful was a huge confidence boost for me."

Helen ate her last bite of roll. "Ah, delicious," she said. "Now, should we talk about the fourth step to becoming a wisdom steward?"

"Sure."

"Great. So have you heard the analogy of the bacon and egg breakfast?"

"Uh, sorry but no."

"Well, in a bacon and egg breakfast the chicken lays the egg for the breakfast. But the pig has to give up its life for the bacon. The chicken is involved, but the pig is committed. As it relates to becoming a wisdom steward, you can't just be casually involved in your improvement actions, you need to commit to improvement. You can't treat it like it's a by-the-way activity. You need to take it seriously. You have to want improvement. Make sense?"

"It does, but right now I'm not sure about what I'm trying to improve upon." Rico said.

"It's alright, that's why you go through the first three steps of self-assessment, reviewing your self-assessment with up to three sharers, and defining what you're going to do about it. You may find you're only one of the personas, say a boaster, or you may find you take on multiple personas depending on the situation. Just make sure that no matter what actions you put in place, you commit to your plan."

"Right, I get what you're saying," Rico said. "But my job is so demanding that I don't know that I can take on more commitments."

Helen brought the cup to her mouth and tipped down the last of the cappuccino. "I get being busy, Rico. Let's say you come up with three things to work on. Start with just one of those three things and commit to improving on that one thing only. Then when you feel like you've mastered that one thing, take on the next thing, then the third. Small, incremental improvements are better than trying to do too much and not doing anything well. Start small, get the win, then move on to the next thing. Got it?"

"I understand," Rico said. "I'm just concerned about putting something else on my plate."

"I had to make it a priority and was able to do it. If it's important enough to you, you'll do it. Now how about you jot down what we talked about?"

Rico took the pen from the clipboard and wrote the hesitator persona definition and characteristics and the fourth step to become a wisdom steward:

BECOMING A WISDOM STEWARD

PERSONA	CHARACTER TRAITS	WHEN IS THIS ME?	WHAT WILL I DO ABOUT IT?
STEWARD – EMBRACING SUCCESS	• GENUINELY SEEKS • CANDIDLY SHARES		
BOASTER – PROVING SUPERIORITY	• SEEKS AND SHARES TO DEMONSTRATE SUPERIORITY TO OTHERS		
HOARDER – BEING COMPETITIVE	• GENUINELY SEEKS • GUARDEDLY SHARES		
POSER – NEEDING TO IMPRESS	• GUARDEDLY SEEKS WITHOUT EXPOSING SELF • SHARES WITHOUT BASIS		
HESITATOR – FEELING SECURE	• GENUINELY SEEKS • SHARES ONLY WHEN IT'S SAFE		

THE STEPS:

1. DEFINE "WHEN IS THIS ME?"
2. REVIEW "WHEN IS THIS ME?" WITH UP TO 3 SHARERS
3. DEFINE "WHAT WILL I DO ABOUT IT?"
4. COMMIT TO YOUR ACTIONS
5.

Helen looked down at her phone. "Great, I just got a message that Rachael is outside waiting for you. Invest in yourself, Rico; you deserve it. Now how about I walk you back?"

"That would be good."

Rico and Helen walked over to Bad Bad Boy; next to the statue stood a small building with the familiar gold door.

"Next time Suomenlinna," Helen said as she opened the door.

"Next time," Rico said.

Rico walked through the door and heard it shut behind him.

"Well, there you are, Rico!"

Funny Boy

Rico stepped out into the warm Sierra Vista weather. He turned to look behind him.

"Huh, Bob the Boaster's house." Rico noticed the gold door on the beige house with red tiled roof.

Beep Beeeeeeep.

Rico turned to the tinny beeping sound to see Rachael leaning on the horn.

"We've got to get going, Rico!" she said.

Rico got to the golf cart and was barely in before Rachael lunged forward.

"Tell me, how has your journey been so far?" Rachael asked.

Rico paused for a minute. "Well, other than the fact I've gone from a home from 40 years ago, to a sunset on the beach to a pink peeing statue in Helsinki, it's been a pretty normal Saturday."

"Funny boy," Rachael said as she sped down the street.

"Where are we going now?" Rico asked.

"You've got one more person to meet. He'll talk with you about the last persona and the fifth step to becoming a wisdom steward."

"Will I be staying in Sierra Vista?"

"Yes, this time you will. Oh and by the way, I have another appointment to tend to, so someone else will be picking you up after you're done."

"Um, that's OK, I think I could just walk home," Rico said.

"I think you'll want to go with the person picking you up."

Rico looked at Rachael, both hands gripping the steering wheel, head forward, gaze straight ahead as if she were driving in the Daytona 500.

"Here we are." Rachael took a hard left into the driveway. Rico looked at the house and its overgrown landscaping, chipped stucco, peeling paint, and cracked tile roof. The only thing that looked new was the gold door at the front of the house.

"Is this it?" Rico asked.

"It is."

"And someone still lives here?"

Rachael smiled. "Yes, now get a move-on."

"Will I see you again?" Rico asked.

"Most probably, now off you go!"

Rico got out of the golf cart and walked to the front door.

"Who's picking me up?" he thought to himself.

"Won't he be surprised," Rachael said as she backed out of the driveway.

Pete the Pontificator

The front door was gold like the others but the wood was weather-beaten and the brass knocker tarnished. A dead aloe vera plant drooped in a pot next to the door. "Enter" was written on a piece of paper taped to the door. Rico turned the doorknob and pushed the door open. He stepped into the foyer, wincing at the smell of cat urine and feces. The only light in the room was from the bright sun straining to shine through the drawn curtains. The room temperature was the same as the outside, amplifying the pungent pet odor. A skinny cat came up to him and rubbed against his bare leg.

"Let's get this over with." Rico heard the gruff voice coming from the corner of the room. A man sat in a dusty brown wingback chair. Rico walked toward the man, the sound of dried cat poop crunched under foot with each step.

"Sit!" The man said, pointing to a wooden stool, already occupied by a cat that hissed at Rico then jumped off. The man picked the cat up.

"Poor baby, are you OK?" he said as he stroked her matted fur.

Rico slowly sat on the stool, able to make out the man's face in the dusky room. His white, leathery face was highlighted by a red bulbous nose with round spectacles positioned halfway down the bridge. The corners of his mouth curved downward, his lower jaw jutted forward, teeth visible like those of a bulldog. What was left of his gray receding hairline was buzz-cut high and tight.

"So you want to talk about being a wisdom steward, eh?" The man asked.

"Um, I guess."

"You guess?" the man barked.

"I mean yes."

"Fine. My name is Pete, not Peter, Petey, or Pedro. Pete."

"What a kook," Rico thought.

"One more thought like that and you're out on your ear!" Pete said.

"Right, the mind reading thing. Sorry, won't happen again." Rico said as he looked down in embarrassment.

"Better not," Pete said as he waved a bony finger at Rico. "Now about being a wisdom steward. I joined the Army straight out of high school. Saw time in Korea and Vietnam. Drove the M46 and M48 Patton tanks. Ended up getting transferred to Fort Huachuca where I served out the rest of my career."

"My dad was a lieutenant colonel at the fort," Rico said.

"What's his name?"

"Well, his name was Alex Brindis. He died a few years ago."

"Brindis? You're Brindis' kid?"

"You knew him?"

"PFFTTT. Now I know why Rachael wanted me to talk to you," Pete said.

"Why?"

"Your dad came to the fort a few years before I retired. Got to work on some special projects with him. Was one of the few who saw my potential. He also gave me some of the best advice I ever got. Just wish I got it years earlier in my career."

"What advice?"

"Go on, baby, get some dinner." Pete kissed the cat, put it on the floor, and watched it scamper off into the kitchen.

"Shortly after he transferred in, I was assigned to help him with modernizing the fort. We held a lot of design discussions with other officers to figure out what that meant and how we should go about doing it. I thought the meetings were going fine, but your dad, he wasn't too happy. Usually, my superiors would just yell at me when something was wrong, but your dad he was different. He sat me down and talked with me. That was something I just wasn't used to."

"What did he say?"

"He told me that our design discussions weren't going well because of me."

"Because of you?" Rico asked.

"That's right, because of me. My first reaction was to tell him to take a flying leap, but I knew enough to not say that to a superior; at least not to his face. So I said, 'What do you mean, Sir?' He said, 'Pete, our job is to understand what it will take to modernize the fort. Our job is to listen. But in meetings you have been talking too much about your own experiences. You're not listening, you're pontificating. It's getting in the way of us learning what we need to do, and you're ticking people off. I'm concerned, Pete, and I want to help you get this right.' Now your old man kind of threw me for a loop. I've never gotten any genuine coaching like what your dad did. He wasn't just telling me what I was doing wrong; he wanted me to get it right."

"That sounds like him, he was always wanting to help me get things right too."

"Yeah, he also told me that others referred to me as Pete the Pontificator, and that they viewed my pontificating as a way of showing I was relevant and to make myself look good. He told me how my blathering on about my war stories didn't just turn people off, it also didn't instill confidence in my superiors that I was promotable. Your dad's words cut through me like a bayonet, but he wasn't wrong."

"My dad certainly didn't mince words."

"No he didn't, and while his coaching was great, for me it was too late. If I had gotten your dad's coaching years ago, I could have gone much higher up the ranks. It's stuck in my craw for years and I can't let it go. Now I'm just an angry old man sitting in this rundown dump--me and my cats."

"Was your career really that bad?" Rico asked.

Pete took a deep breath. "In the early days it was OK, but as I got older I watched younger men and women pass me up in the ranks; people I had trained in basic became my superiors. Was my pontificating the only reason I was passed up? Probably not, but it certainly didn't help. Now, should we talk about the fifth step to becoming a wisdom steward?"

"Yes," Rico said.

"As you can probably tell, getting feedback was always tough for me. When your old man told me about my pontificating and needing to make changes, he also told me it wasn't enough to commit to making a change; but I had to get feedback to ensure the changes I committed to make actually stuck. He made me get feedback over a three-month period from him and two other officers. What made it really tough was that both of those officers were at one time below me in the chain of command, so I had to really suck it up and hear hard messages from people I used to yell at. I hated it at first, but I also realize now that if I hadn't had that regular feedback, I probably wouldn't have made the changes I needed."

Pete paused for a moment. "Rico, I've seen a lot of people just like you come through here, and I'm sure they've left thinking what a jerk I was. And they were right; I was a jerk and I was fully prepared to be a jerk with you. That is until I heard you were Brindis' kid. You're still young and can make the needed changes to become a wisdom steward. Don't squander the opportunity."

"Thank you," Rico said.

"Now how about you get to writing."

Rico took the pen from the clipboard and wrote the pontificator persona definition and characteristics and the fifth step to become a wisdom steward:

BECOMING A WISDOM STEWARD

PERSONA	CHARACTER TRAITS	WHEN IS THIS ME?	WHAT WILL I DO ABOUT IT?
STEWARD – EMBRACING SUCCESS	• GENUINELY SEEKS • CANDIDLY SHARES		
BOASTER – PROVING SUPERIORITY	• SEEKS AND SHARES TO DEMONSTRATE SUPERIORITY TO OTHERS		
HOARDER – BEING COMPETITIVE	• GENUINELY SEEKS • GUARDEDLY SHARES		
POSER – NEEDING TO IMPRESS	• GUARDEDLY SEEKS WITHOUT EXPOSING SELF • SHARES WITHOUT BASIS		
HESITATOR – FEELING SECURE	• GENUINELY SEEKS • SHARES ONLY WHEN IT'S SAFE		
PONTIFICATOR – STAYING RELEVANT	• DOESN'T SEEK • SELECTIVELY SHARES TO MAKE SELF LOOK GOOD		

THE STEPS:

1. DEFINE "WHEN IS THIS ME?"
2. REVIEW "WHEN IS THIS ME?" WITH UP TO 3 SHARERS
3. DEFINE "WHAT WILL I DO ABOUT IT?"
4. COMMIT TO YOUR ACTIONS
5. ASSESS PROGRESS OVER 3 MONTHS

"Now, get going, someone is waiting for you outside."

Rico stood up just as a cat jumped into Pete's lap.

"Thank you for the conversation, Pete, and the kind words about my dad."

Pete nuzzled with the cat as it rubbed its head on Pete's cheek. Rico walked to the door and looked back to see Pete engrossed in his pet. Rico opened the door to see the golf cart and its driver.

"It can't be," Rico said.

Pete looked up at Rico and smiled as he walked out the door. "It is."

Defining Moment

R ico slowly walked closer to the golf cart. "Dad?"

"My boy."

"But . . . how . . . ?"

Alex smiled. "Get in, Rico."

Rico sat on the golf cart bench, keeping his gaze on his father the entire time.

"Dad, how is this happening?"

"It's OK, Rico. Let's just talk." Alex backed out of the driveway and started driving.

"How long are you here?"

"Not long."

Rico paused, not sure how to best use the time.

"Dad, I'm so sorry I didn't call you on your birthday." Rico thought back to his last interaction before Alex died.

"I know. Had I known I was going to pass the next day I would have been gentler with you. I didn't mean to leave you with such guilt."

"Dad . . . I . . ."

"Rico, you know how much I love you."

Rico started to cry. "I know, I love you too."

"Rico, I'm so proud of you and the man you've grown into. Your growth journey isn't over, though. There are some things you need to work on, to become an even better man than you are today. This afternoon you've heard stories about people who were out of balance in their ability to genuinely seek and candidly share wisdom. Each of them had an epiphany, a defining moment which helped them get on the path to being a wisdom steward. You're out of balance, Rico. This is your defining moment. Do you understand?"

Rico choked back tears. "Yes."

"I know what you're made of, that you'll do the right thing. Genuinely seek and candidly share. That's what wisdom stewards do."

"I understand, Dad."

"Good, Rico."

Rico paused for a moment. "Dad, there's one more thing."

"What's that?"

"When I was 16 I . . . "

Alex interrupted. "Took 20 dollars from my wallet."

"You knew about that?"

Alex smiled. "What, you think I wasn't a 16-year-old once? You don't know half of what I did growing up."

"Man, I loved that house," Alex said as the golf cart pulled up to Rico's mother's house. "Remember, genuinely seek and candidly share. That's what wisdom stewards do."

Rico looked down, searching for what else to say to his father.

"Kiss your mom for me," Alex said.

"I will," Rico said as he looked up just as his father faded away.

"Dad? Dad?"

He put his head in his hands, alone in the golf cart.

Eventful

Rico sat in the golf cart, thinking about all that happened throughout the afternoon. His father's words about genuinely seeking and candidly sharing wisdom. Then there were the words of advice from Bob, Herman, Priscilla, Helen, and Pete.

Embrace the journey.

There's no easy path to success.

You've got this.

Invest in yourself.

Don't squander the opportunity.

"This was supposed to be a lazy Sierra Vista trip," Rico said to himself. "No idea I'd be in for the ride of my life, that I'd get to see Dad one more time."

Rico smiled, then got out of the golf cart and walked up the driveway. His mother opened the door just as Rico approached the front door.

"How was your walk, Rico?"

"Eventful," Rico said as he kissed his mother.

"That's from Dad."

"Oh, Rico," she said as she hugged him.

"I'll put the golf cart in the street so you can get out of the garage."

"What golf cart?" She asked.

Rico turned around to see the empty spot in the driveway.

Monday Afternoon

On Monday afternoon Rico was getting ready to drive back to Phoenix. He had put hours into his lessons-learned document he would present to Alma the next morning. He decided to complete the wisdom steward sheet Rachael gave him as input to his learnings. He discovered that his most prevalent personas were the boaster, hoarder, and poser. He was a boaster and hoarder mostly with his colleagues and a poser with his bosses. To get on the path to being a wisdom steward, he was going to have to do three things:

1. Stop trying to act superior to others
2. Be willing to humbly share, even if it meant talking about things he did wrong

3. Let his actions impress his bosses and stop trying to dazzle them with words.

BECOMING A WISDOM STEWARD

PERSONA	CHARACTER TRAITS	WHEN IS THIS ME?	WHAT WILL I DO ABOUT IT?
STEWARD – EMBRACING SUCCESS	• GENUINELY SEEKS • CANDIDLY SHARES	NEVER	NO POSER, BOASTER OR HOARDER
BOASTER – PROVING SUPERIORITY	• SEEKS AND SHARES TO DEMONSTRATE SUPERIORITY TO OTHERS	WITH COLLEAGUES	FORGET ABOUT SUPERIORITY
HOARDER – BEING COMPETITIVE	• GENUINELY SEEKS • GUARDEDLY SHARES	WITH COLLEAGUES	SHARE HUMBLY
POSER – NEEDING TO IMPRESS	• GUARDEDLY SEEKS WITHOUT EXPOSING SELF • SHARES WITHOUT BASIS	WITH BOSSES	STOP TRYING TO IMPRESS MY BOSSES
HESITATOR – FEELING SECURE	• GENUINELY SEEKS • SHARES ONLY WHEN IT'S SAFE	NEVER	NO ACTION
PONTIFICATOR – STAYING RELEVANT	• DOESN'T SEEK • SELECTIVELY SHARES TO MAKE SELF LOOK GOOD	NEVER	NO ACTION

THE STEPS:

1. DEFINE "WHEN IS THIS ME?"
2. REVIEW "WHEN IS THIS ME?" WITH UP TO 3 SHARERS
3. DEFINE "WHAT WILL I DO ABOUT IT?"
4. COMMIT TO YOUR ACTIONS
5. ASSESS PROGRESS OVER 3 MONTHS

His next steps were to ask three people to review his self-assessment and confirm his actions. He decided to ask Alma, his peer Tami, and Chin, another project manager in the group, to be his three sharers. Their job was to observe Rico's actions and supportively speak the truth to him when he wasn't walking the wisdom steward talk.

Tuesday morning, Rico waited outside Alma's office, ready for his discussion, the words *genuinely seek, candidly share* ringing in his head.

Five Years Later

Rico sat in his cubicle looking over the training report numbers. The wisdom steward course he created three years ago had become the most popular training course in the company, helping those from the CEO on down become wisdom stewards. He pulled out a spiral-bound notebook from his desk drawer that had *Genuinely Seek, Candidly Share* written across the cover. Through the five-year journey, Rico had recorded his thoughts, concerns, successes and failures. He pulled out a yellow marker and flipped through the pages, highlighting some of his most impactful learnings:

May 29, 2018 — Just got out of meeting with Alma where I reviewed my lessons-learned and how I was going to stop being a boaster, hoarder, and poser. She acknowledged my courageous transparency and supported my plan. While her words were appreciated, I still felt like a total loser. I hated admitting that I had things to work on.

May 31, 2018 – *Just finished meeting with Alma, Tami and Chin. They're all happy to be sharers to help me on my wisdom steward journey. They couldn't have been more gracious and welcoming. This still really hurts to have to do this.*

July 11, 2018 – *Chin pulled me aside after a staff meeting and told me that I was being a boaster with one of my colleagues. I thought I was candidly sharing, but she pointed out that my sharing was interpreted as trying to prove I was right about something and that everyone else was wrong. Sometimes I get it but there are other times where I just seem to have blind spots. Still more work to do.*

January 8, 2019 – *Alma asked me to give a lessons-learned presentation to our entire organization on the Apollo project. I reviewed my first draft with Alma and she asked me how candidly I was sharing about not just the successes but the budget and schedule miss. I reworked the* *slide deck. It was really hard admitting that I made mistakes in front of so many people, but I was amazed at the amount of positive feedback I received afterward. I even had a few people tell me how courageous I was to get up in front of the group and be so candid and transparent. Made me feel really good.*

June 18, 2020 – *Alma asked me if I'd be interested in being a wisdom sharer to Greg. He's a boaster, hoarder and poser just like I was. He and I just met. Man, he's got a lot to learn. Just like looking in a mirror.*

August 24, 2020 – *Just got off a Zoom meeting with Greg. He's making good progress. It's also a great reinforcement to me in candidly sharing as well as not slipping back into my old boaster, hoarder, and poser habits. I just wish we could meet in person. This dang COVID-19!*

May 26, 2021 – *It's been three years since my golf cart experience in Sierra Vista. I just finished meeting up with Alice, who is a big-time hesitator. She's the tenth person Alma has sent my way to be a wisdom sharer coach. Alma* told me she would be meeting with the CEO next week about developing a wisdom steward training course . . . and she wants me to head it up. Yikes!

June 4, 2021 – Well, it's official, I'm now assigned to work part-time with our learning and development organization to develop a wisdom steward course. Kind of exciting and scary at the same time.

January 17, 2022 – We just launched the training course. Ten attendees. One is a real pontificator. He's going to be a real challenge!

March 29, 2022 – How embarrassing, I slipped back into my old ways and was a boaster in a staff meeting. It's so important that I keep being a wisdom steward at the top of my mind so I don't relapse into my old ways.

September 29, 2022 – Just got an email from one of the course attendees. He told me about his journey from poser to steward and how he and another poser from the class are coaching each other. It's so cool to see people helping each other to be wisdom stewards!

Rico flipped to the next blank page and wrote:

June 19, 2023 – Just got the report from learning and development that the wisdom steward course is the most popular course in the company. What a journey it's been! Today I highlighted some of most foundational events over the past five years. I wonder what the next five will bring?

Rico closed the notebook, brushed his hand across the cover, and put it back in the drawer just as Alma walked up.

"Nice job on the wisdom steward course," she said. "My boss just went to it and asked me to help him stop being a pontificator. He told me it was OK to share that with you because he'd like you to help him too."

"I'd be happy to," Rico said.

"Good. See you at the all-hands later."

As Alma left, Rico looked at the wisdom steward clipboard that hung on the cubicle's wall next to a picture of his father.

"I'm in balance, Dad," he said as he tacked the training report next to the picture.

See a sample chapter from *Behind Gold Doors-Nine Crucial Elements to Achieve Good-Enough Contentment*

At This Time...

Ty got his morning coffee and turned on his computer. The first email was from one of the companies where he had sent his resume. He hovered the cursor over the email, took a deep breath, and double-tapped the track pad, opening the email.

Dear Mr. Taylor:

Thank you so much for your interest in Lake Industries. At this time...

Ty closed the email without reading further. They all started out with something like *"at this time," "unfortunately,"* or *"we currently don't."* They ended with an empty *"we will keep your resume on file should something become available which matches your skillset. Thank you for your interest in blah-di-blah company."* He had gotten dozens of them, each one like a slug to the gut. Just as he shut his laptop Kate came into the kitchen. She immediately could tell what had happened.

"I'm so sorry, Ty," Kate said as she came around to him and put her hand on his shoulder. "Something will turn up; you just need to be patient."

Ty took a sip of coffee. "It's been six months and not one bite. Severance is gone, and the pittance we get from unemployment runs out next week. How much more patient do I need to be?"

"I wish I knew, honey. We're doing okay on finances and I've got plenty of client work in backlog. We've been through tougher times than this and we got through it. We'll get through this too." Kate poured herself a cup of coffee in a travel mug and took her lunch out of the fridge. "We'll talk more tonight, honey; I believe in you."

"I'm so lucky to have you," Ty said. "Do you want a lift to the train station?"

"I'll walk this morning, but how about you pick me up tonight? I should be on the 5:40, I'll call you if not."

"Got it, I love you."

Kate leaned over to kiss Ty. "Love you too."

Kate headed down the hallway to the front door. Ty heard the door open then gently click shut as she left.

His routine was the same every day. After Kate left for work, he'd finish going through his email inbox, then cruise the news websites, then up for a shower, then onto the job websites. As the weeks went by and the rejections piled up, he cast his job search net wider and wider; even looking at jobs that new college grads could do. He spent hours each day looking at opportunities, trying to network, and responding to job postings. Sometimes after lunch he would break routine and just sit on the couch with a bowl of chips watching afternoon talk shows. The couch sessions increased in frequency as he became more and more depressed. Most times he just wore sweats, since his pants had become too tight, but he knew better than to wear something with an elastic waistband if he and Kate were going out. He'd do the best he could to squeeze into his pants, preferring hooks over snaps to avoid them popping under pressure.

Socializing with friends was the worst. "How's the job search coming?" He'd hear it over and over. "Just great, pursuing a couple of opportunities," he'd lie, then try to change the topic. He particularly hated having to face his daughters and his shame of feeling like such a loser-unemployed dad.

Ty finished up his morning activities then made himself a tuna sandwich with chips and soda. "Wonder what's on TV this afternoon?" he said. "No, I need to work." He looked at his laptop, then the TV remote, then back at the laptop. "Actually, I need to get out." He finished his lunch, got his jacket and left the house for a walk.

"It's a beautiful Fall day," Ty said to himself as he walked down the street towards the train station. It was about a mile walk, one that he used to do every day when he worked at Conset, and the same that Kate did each day to get to her office. The street was lined with reddish-yellow trees that rained leaves onto the ground with each gust of wind. Ty took deep breaths as he walked, feeling the cool Autumn air fill his lungs. He walked by the park next to the train station. Two mothers with strollers sat on a bench talking. A man played fetch with his dog; on each throw the dog would run as fast as he could to the ball, kicking up a trail of leaves with each lunge. As he got closer to the train station, he noticed an old woman sitting in a wheelchair next to a bench. He slowed his walk to look at her. She wore a huge hat adorned with white flowers, a pink polka-dot sweater, and red and orange striped pants. On her lap sat a large paisley-print carpet bag. Her makeup looked as if it were applied with a putty knife. Her sunken eyes stared at Ty as he walked by, expressionless in her gaze, even though Ty smiled at her as he passed. As he continued to the station, he turned to look at the woman, who was still ogling him. Ty quickened his pace to get out of her eyeshot.

"Think I'll go into the city," Ty said to himself as he arrived at the train station. "I can make the 1:05, get into Chicago by 2, then Kate and I can ride the 5:40 back together.". He loved walking along Lakeshore Drive and experiencing the sights, smells and sounds of the expansive Lake Michigan. He bought a ticket and waited on the platform for the train to Union Station. The train's horn broke the silence of the Fall day as it approached the station; followed by the grinding of the metal wheels on the track as the train slowly approached the platform. He stood to board the train as it came to a stop. "How odd," he said to himself. The car was a familiar dingy silver, weathered by the countless trips around Chicagoland. What wasn't so typical were the doors--gleaming gold, looking as if they were just delivered from the foundry and installed that day. The doors slid open, Ty boarded, then with a whoosh the doors closed behind him. He looked up and down the empty car and sat down in the seat next to the doors. Ty pulled out his phone, waiting for the train to depart. Just then the door abruptly opened.

"Help me!" Ty heard as he turned and looked back at the door.

See a sample from *Behind Gold Doors-Five Legends Offer the Keys to Empowering Leadership*

Embossed Card

Sam had been dreading this meeting for days. He stood outside Karen's office waiting for her to finish her phone conversation. He could see her through the window in her door. She held up her index finger. Only one more minute before the dressing-down.

Karen hung up the phone and motioned Sam in.

"How's it going?" Sam said.

"Fine, thanks."

Karen got up from her desk and sat at a small round table with two chairs. Sam sat across from her and put his notebook and water bottle on the table.

"Sam, have you had a chance to review your performance appraisal?"

Sam opened his notebook. In it was a folded copy of the appraisal.

"I have."

"Good. Let's talk through strengths and areas for improvement."

Sam had always been an over-achiever. Graduating from college at age 20, he took great pride in how much he achieved at such a young age. He had been considered a rising star at the company since joining five years earlier. He was recently promoted to a management position, with an organization of ten people reporting to him. This was his first performance appraisal as a manager.

"So, let's first go through strengths," Karen said. Sam barely looked at the strengths, it was that one area for improvement that dominated his thoughts.

Karen continued. "Great delivery results, you come in on budget, customer satisfaction exceeds expectations. Great work." Karen continued with more specifics and comments from customers. Sam sat quietly as she talked, giving an occasional nod and *mm-hmm* to signal understanding.

"Enough with this, get on with the meat," he thought.

"Great, now let's talk about areas for improvement."

Sam leaned back in his chair, his hands gripping the armrests.

"Your organization's employee satisfaction surveys raised something we need to work on together."

Sam looked back at his manager score on the appraisal where his score was compared to other managers in the company. His score was among the lowest, with 95 percent of the managers scoring higher than him. It was the first time in his career he wasn't at the top of the heap, let alone being in the lowest five percent.

"In looking at the questions and comments, people seem concerned about your ability to empower others."

This was a total shock to Sam. He thought he did a great job of delegating and getting things done with his team. It wasn't just one person who said he didn't delegate effectively; it was a consensus among his team.

"I just don't understand this," Sam stammered. "I work so hard to make sure I am delegating work effectively." Karen and Sam continued to talk through the employee survey. To Karen, this was something for Sam to work on in his leadership journey. To Sam, it was like having bamboo stuck under his fingernails. Karen saw how this was impacting Sam; so she decided to make him an offer.

"Sam, you have great potential, and I want to ensure I'm doing my part to help you grow as a leader." Karen got up from the table, went back to her desk, opened the top drawer, took out a gold card, and sat back down at the table.

"There is a very special empowerment class I would like you to attend," Karen said as she handed him the card.

Sam looked at the card, a gold embossed door on the front, an address on the back. He recognized the address.

"This is a bakery; you want me to go to a class at a bakery?"

"Take tomorrow off. Go to the address on the card. They'll be waiting for you."

"Um, okay," Sam said. He had thought for sure he would be fired. Instead he was being sent to a class. Sam got up from the table, grateful he still had his job but perplexed by the gold card and what awaited him the next day.

"Thank you, Karen."

"Hang in there Sam, and let's get together after the class to talk about what you've learned."

"Okay." Sam left her office. As he walked to his office, he ran his thumb over the outline of the door on the embossed card. He flipped it over and looked at the address again.

"A bakery?"

See more at ***behindgolddoors.com***

See a sample from *Behind Gold Doors-Seven Steps to Create a Disability Inclusive Organization*

Rain Gear

For the rest of the day Jade couldn't get Kelly's story out of her mind. She had never known anyone close to her with a disability and couldn't imagine the pain Kelly felt watching her father die the way he did.

"*How could I possibly do this justice?*" she thought to herself. "*I'm an engineer, I build stuff. I don't have the experience to do this. What if I fail? I don't want to disappoint Kelly, knowing how important this is to her.*" Jade got up to get some water. On the way she looked outside at the dark clouds forming. "*Gonna need the rain gear tonight,*" she thought.

At 5:30 p.m. she packed up her stuff, slipped on her rain pants and jacket, and headed out. She walked by Kelly's office just as Kelly looked up and gave Jade a quick wave goodbye.

It was unusually dark for this time of year. The rain quickly went from a light mist to a torrential downpour. Jade had ridden in rain before, but nothing quite like this. "*Just go slow,*" she thought as she went through each intersection. She considered stopping and waiting it out, but there was no guarantee that it would let up. "*Halfway home. I can do this.*"

Then it happened.

Acknowledgements

Behind Gold Doors: Five Easy Steps to Become a Wisdom Steward was a fun book to research and write. Heartfelt thanks to Darren Ellis, Lori Lake, Mike Burkhalter, Daniel Adent, Jeanne Parish, Leo Ahearn, Keith Krell, Matt Pacelli, and Kay Gill. Special thanks to my editor and wife Patty Pacelli for the hours of reading, reviewing, cleaning up my bad English, and wise counsel. Each contribution made the manuscript more interesting and credible. My deepest thanks to each of you.

Thanks for the Outstanding insights Leo!

Lonnie

More Books by Lonnie Pacelli

Want to be a leader others admire? Get the 12 simple leadership lessons the best leaders crush in *Why Don't They Follow Me?*

Want to be more disability inclusive but don't know where to start? You need the seven steps in *Behind Gold Doors-Seven Steps to Create a Disability Inclusive Organization*

Need to deliver projects on time, budget, and within scope? Get 100 lessons to make you a better project manager in *Six-Word Lessons for Project Managers*

Want to know how to avoid the project guillotine? Get 100 lessons to avert failure in *Six-Word Lessons to Avoid Project Disaster*

Want to know what it really means to be a great project sponsor? See how and more in the *Project Management Screw-Ups Series*

Are you guilty of the seven deadly sins of leadership? See this and more in the *Straight Talk Leadership Seminars*

Want to be the type of leader who people *want* to follow? Get 75 lessons the best leaders use to deliver results in *Lead Already!*

See Lonnie's Amazon Backlist at LonnieOnAmazon.com.

See more about Lonnie at LonniePacelli.com